MAKERS OF THE WOMEN'S INSTITUTE

Profiles of Adelaide Hoodless, Madge Watt, Lady Denman,

Grace Hadow, Lady Brunner and Cicely McCall

Ernie Richards

MAKERS OF THE WOMEN'S INSTITUTE

CONTENTS

Introduction

This booklet is a brief introduction to the life and work of six of the most influential women in the history of the WI.

The first two were Canadian and were responsible for starting the WI: Adelaide Hoodless in Canada, then Madge Watt who brought the movement to Britain, and then ultimately to the world. The other four women are British: the first, and longest serving Chair of the NFWI, gave her name to the WI College - Lady Denman, and her Vice-Chairman who served with her for 22 years was Grace Hadow.

The remaining two women are the longest lived NFWI Officers: the actress turned voluntary worker Elizabeth Irving who became Lady Brunner and lived till she was 99, and the incredible Cicely McCall who made voluntary work into a full time job and who lived till she was 103.

For some, the WI was their entire life. For others, it was shared by other interests. For Adelaide Hoodless from the moment her son died, she dedicated her life to helping all girls and mothers understand the principles of hygiene and keeping their families safe. Madge Watt enjoyed her life as a writer, the wife of a doctor, and populariser of WIs created earlier by Adelaide. When her husband died, she came to Britain and again devoted all her energies to starting WI groups here, and then later world-wide.

Lady Denman had a very full social life and a husband and children, until she met the WI. Then she served it with passion and dedication. She had other interests which she pursued with equal vigour.

Grace Hadow began as a lover and teacher of literature. For her, the WI was an extension of this life-long passion. She never lost her first love, and tried to persuade all her WI members to share her love for this life-enhancing and mind-broadening joy.

Elizabeth Irving all her life was devoted to the theatre and acting. For her, the WI was a natural part of this kind of communicating, and again like Grace, she wanted everyone to share her passion.

Cicely McCall was a woman of many parts, who was interested primarily in social and psychiatric care-work. She had two spells serving the WI, one as Educational Adviser and the other as Principal of Denman. To these, she brought her understanding of people's needs to the service of WI members. Whatever people's starting point, however limited their vision or however limited their abilities physical or mental, they all need reassurance and affirmation that yes, this is possible for them – yes, you can do this.

The urgency of getting the work done drove several of these women to appear sometimes to be brusque, possibly to the point of rudeness. I think Madge and Cicely never suffered fools gladly, and were often impatient with the slowness of the people they had to work with. For Trudie, Grace, and Elizabeth, keeping people on board with whatever plans they had was paramount, and they all showed infinite patience.

These six women, though all completely different in personality and experience, shared one characteristic: they created new things where there was nothing before. Adelaide in Canada, Madge in Britain, followed by Trudie, Grace, Elizabeth and Cicely – all created a movement, extended it, expanded it, made it relevant to their own times. They were not made by the WI – they made the WI.

What is staggering to take in is not just the effort involved in taking news of the WI around the country – first Canada and then the UK – but the number of miles covered by these pioneers. First, Addie with huge journeys by horse-driven carriage, Madge the same in Canada and then later in Britain and then Cicely in her Morris motor car, visiting every county in England and Wales bar one.

At the end of this booklet, I give a list of books where you can learn more about these astonishing women.

In Centenary year – 2015 – it seems even more vital that we should all understand how the movement started and developed and who made these developments happen.

These are the women who set the foundations which made the WI what it is today.

Adelaide Hoodless

(1857 – 1910)

John Harold Hoodless was only 14 months old when he fell ill and died. The doctor said his death was probably caused by drinking contaminated milk. His mother, Adelaide Hoodless, married to a furniture manufacturer, and living in a well-ordered house, was appalled that it was her ignorance of basic hygiene that had led to the death of her son.

She determined to do something about it.

That 'something' triggered the start of what became an unstoppable expansion of women's organisations that now spans four continents, 108 countries and has 7 million members.

Adelaide Hoodless could never have dreamed when she opened the very first WI in the world at Stoney Creek, Ontario, that it would develop into such an enormous size. Even in her native Canada, by 1965 there were 3,350 WIs with a membership of 72,000. But the death of John Harold at 14 months made Adelaide aware of the need to teach herself and then others of the vital importance of understanding food – its preservation and cooking, because literally the lives of her children were in her hands.

Adelaide was the last of 13 children, born in 1857 to David Hamilton a farmer and his wife Jane. Several months before Adelaide was born, David died. Adelaide learned the hard way how to share the running of a farm without a father. She learned the two most valuable lessons anyone can learn: how to be independent and how to co-operate with others. She was given her tasks to do and she had to do them often alone rain or shine, and these tasks increased as she grew older. But there is so much work to be done on a farm that everyone needs to help everyone else and learn how to share the labour. Adelaide had only a basic education but she had a keen mind and developed her studies by wide and deep reading. She read ancient and modern philosophers. Her favourite was Herbert Spencer, a Victorian English philosopher and sociologist, and her favourite quotation from him was:

'The goodness of a society ultimately depends on the nature of its citizens and since the nature of its citizens is more modifiable by early training than by anything else, we must conclude that the welfare of the family underlines the welfare of society.' And she carried out this principle right through her life.

In 1881 Adelaide married John Hoodless, a manufacturer and dealer in furniture and they went to live in a luxurious home in Hamilton. They had four children, John Harold was the youngest. When her doctor told her that John had probably died from drinking contaminated milk, she was shocked to realise that she had not understood enough about basic hygiene to stop this happening. She was even more shocked to learn that many babies were dying of the same cause – one in five babies died before the age of five. Soon she was heading a campaign against the selling of impure milk in Hamilton.

At the same time, she realised that to prevent things like this happening in the future, all girls should be taught food hygiene as part of their schooling. The idea of teaching what became known as domestic science was born. This was the first of the many battles that she fought in her comparatively short life.

Adelaide believed it was wrong to educate boys and girls along the same lines. She felt that the education system was making home-breakers rather than home-makers, that there was a distinct role for girls to fulfil and that the curriculum should be shaped so that they were taught the essentials of hygiene and managing a home.

Between 1893 and 1908 Addie succeeded in having domestic science courses introduced into 32 schools – but only after a heroic struggle. Her son spoke of her ordeal:

'Today one can hardly conceive that the attacks made upon her could have occurred. She was derided in the press and from the platform as one of those despised "new women"." Let her stay at home and take care of her family" a lot of people said.' But it was because she was concerned about her own family that she wanted to involve other families in learning about disease and how to prevent their children dying. She said, 'Apart from my family duties, the education of mothers has been my life's work.'

But more courses in schools meant there had to be more teachers, so Addie set about starting the Ontario Normal School of Domestic Science and Art, originally set up in the Y.W.C.A. in Hamilton. So many girls wanted to train as teachers that it had to expand, and Addie got the money from Sir William Macdonald to set up the Macdonald Institute on the campus of the Ontario Agricultural College at Guelph, Ontario.

She was asked to prepare a text book in Domestic Science, which was published in 1898. This 'little red book' as it was called, was far ahead of its time with calorie charts, chemical analysis and the importance of meat, fruit and fresh vegetables in the diet.

Addie had always been interested in Hamilton Y.W.C.A. and its potential to teach girls better methods in household work. She was President of the Hamilton Y.W.C.A. and led the delegation of 60 Canadian women at the Colombian Exposition in Chicago in 1893 and saw then that the work needed putting on a national basis. When she came back to Hamilton she set about this task:

'I wrote to every city and town in Canada. Where there were already established Y.W.C.A.s, I asked for their views: where I did not know of any existing, I wrote to the Mayor of the place asking for information and if he would kindly place the letter in the hands of some responsible Christian woman, who would help me in my efforts to get information. In all I sent out 90 letters: some were most courteously answered, some were ignored. The result was that on 7th December 1893 we held our first national conference in the Y.W.C.A. building in Toronto.'

In 1897 as a National Officer in the National Council of Women, Addie helped Lady Aberdeen in the formation of the Victorian Order of Nurses, to commemorate the Jubilee of Queen Victoria. She worked at this tirelessly for she knew that this group of nurses would bring into women in their homes the basic facts of hygiene and nutrition.

But, also in 1897, Addie was involved in an even more far-reaching campaign: the setting up of the first WI in the world.

Addie gave a speech at the Agricultural College at Guelph, about the need to train girls in domestic science and sewing.

'Girls should be educated to fit them for the sphere of life for which they were destined – that of home-maker, and this should be done by teaching Domestic Science in our publicly-owned schools.'

In the audience was a Mr Erland Lee, a young farmer and secretary of the Farmers' Institute of Saltfleet Township – an organisation for men. But they did have the occasional ladies' night, when wives could come – with their husbands. Erland Lee invited Addie to come and speak at his next ladies' night – to the dismay of most of his members. There were 35 wives present when Addie suggested that the women, like the men, should have their own Institute. When she asked how many women would be interested in setting up their own Institute, 35 hands went up. A meeting was organised for February 17th and on that incredible stormy night word had spread amongst the farmers' wives and 101 women came plus 1 man – Mr Lee, who chaired the meeting until officers had been elected then took a back seat.

In her speech Addie pointed out that if men needed an organisation and it helped them grow better crops of hay, grain and fruit and produced better livestock, then an institute for women would be equally helpful in their work. Indeed, she said, it was much more necessary since women's work – home craft and motherhood - was more important than that of the men as it concerned the home and care of the loved ones who lived there. A name was chosen for the organisation and a committee was elected with Addie as Honorary President.

At their next meeting a constitution was drawn up and a statement of aims. But this was much more than teaching a knowledge of hygiene: their aims were huge and ambitious. The aims of the Institute were:

'To promote that knowledge of Household Science which shall lead to improvement in household architecture with special attention to home sanitation; to a better understanding of the economic and hygienic value of foods and fuels, and to a more scientific care of children with a view to raising the general standard of the health of our people'

The Institute interests would be divided into six branches:

1 Domestic economy.
2 Architecture with special reference to sanitation, heat, light, etc.
3 Physiology, hygiene, medicine, calisthenics, etc.

4 Floriculture and horticulture.

5 Music and art.

6 Literature and sociology, education and legislation.

What a programme! Of course, like most job specifications, this is an impossibly ambitious curriculum to fulfil. But how marvellous at their first real meeting to decide on these aims. It constantly gave them goals to strive for. The amazing thing is that although this was drawn up in 1897 in Canada, it is still the basis of all WI activities. And, of course, all these subjects are taught at the WI College – Denman.

The first three subjects are the basis of Addie's work and the WIs that were formed in Canada or later in Great Britain.

Floriculture and horticulture represent women's interest in growing things and also the start of the decorative arts. Music, art and literature are there not only for sheer enjoyment, but also as contributing enormously to the creativity of children and adults and to the understanding of people and relationships.

The last three subjects listed: sociology, education and legislation represent the start of the preparation for citizenship which WIs have always known they needed.

So started the very first WI.

They spread rapidly throughout Ontario and then the rest of Canada and then to Britain.

In 1899 Addie came to London as Canadian delegate to the International Congress of the Council of Women. She spoke on 'technical education' for girls and mentioned in passing the Women's Institutes of Canada. She writes afterwards about the speech and its reception:

'I was able to tell the English women that the organisation had been recognised by the government as of value to the state. It was astonishing how this organisation appealed to the old country people (her British audience.) I was deluged with enquiries, even from such important leaders of the agricultural movement as Lady Warwick. At that conference I heard reports from many nations and not one reported such an organisation for women in the rural districts as the Women's Institutes of Ontario. So you see we are truly pioneers in this great movement.'

She was the person who understood that when you teach girls and women how to run a home, you are teaching more than just technical skills: you are teaching them how to live and how to ensure that their family live full lives.

'Domestic Science,' she said, 'is the application of scientific principles to the management of the home. It teaches the value of pure air, proper food, systematic management, economy, care of children, domestic and civil sanitation and the prevention of disease. It calls for higher ideals of home life and more respect for domestic occupations. In short, it is a direct education for women as home-makers. But the woman in doing this is always doing more than the pure technical aspects of the work. She is helping to shape character.

'The management of the home has more to do in the moulding of character than any other influence, owing to the large place it fills in the early life of the individual during the most plastic stage of development. We are, therefore, justified in an effort to secure a place for home economics, or domestic science, in the educational institutions of this country.'

'A nation cannot rise above the level of its homes, therefore women must work and study together to raise our homes to the highest possible level.'

She was a firm believer that:

'No higher vocation has been, or ever will be, given to women than that of Home-maker and Citizen Builder.'

Addie was single minded and determined. She herself had no academic aspirations and therefore never went beyond fighting for domestic science courses in schools and in training colleges.

In her own public life, she demonstrated citizenship herself, but was too busy with the home and everything it included, to develop either high academic achievement for women or the cultivation of citizenship skills on a regular basis. This would be left to others to do – academic achievement by Grace Hadow and citizenship by Madge Watt. But what a start Addie gave them and everyone else in the movement.

She died at a comparatively early age – on the eve of her 53rd birthday, while making a public speech about her passion: domestic science and the empowerment of women.

Madge Watt

(1868 – 1948)

The second determined woman in the history of the WI was also a Canadian but Madge, faced with the creation of WIs by Addie in 1897 and believing so passionately in them, set herself the target of getting them going in Great Britain. Not content with that she then set herself another target – making the movement go round the whole world.

She was born Margaret Rose Robertson in 1868 to parents who were Canadian-born children of Scottish settlers. Her father was a QC and Madge inherited his logical and clear thinking mind.

Madge went to Toronto University and was one of the first women to be awarded an MA degree in 1890. From then until 1907 she earned a reasonable living in newspapers writing stories and sketches. She was hailed as a representative of the 'New Woman,' made famous by Ibsen and George Bernard Shaw, because in her writing she used themes created by feminist thinkers. But she was careful not to suggest that women should break away from their family life and obligations.

Although she felt that the institution of marriage needed reform, she married Doctor Alfred Tennyson Watt in 1893 and later bore him two sons.

Her husband was Chief Medical Officer, Superintendent of Quarantine for the Province of British Columbia. She joined the Metchosin WI in 1909 and flung herself into the movement. She organised WIs in British Columbia under the Department of Agriculture. She was secretary to the first Advisory Board of Women (Department of Agriculture British Columbia) ever set up in a Government Department of Canada. This later served as a model for other provinces of Canada.

In 1912 Madge was chosen to represent the city of Victoria in the University Commission. The same year she was elected President of the University Women's Clubs of Vancouver Island. In the following year, she represented the Government of British Columbia at the International Farming Congress and was elected Honorary Secretary of the National Council of Women's Institutes in Canada.

She seemed to be completely settled in her life as wife, mother, organiser of WIs and a highly successful speaker and writer.

But then catastrophe.

In 1913 her husband was accused of being involved in a scandal. Although he was subsequently cleared of any involvement, the strain of the investigation took its toll and he killed himself. Madge could not face the thought of staying in Canada and decided to take her sons to England, where no-one would know them.

When war broke out the following year and men were recruited into the army, it meant that women had to take their place and do the work on the land. Madge realised that all their individual efforts needed co-ordinating and that women needed to work with the Department of Agriculture to increase food production. She suggested to the Department of Agriculture that they should develop WIs on the Canadian model, and she used her own experience of the Metchosin WI as a blue print. She gave many speeches on these lines throughout the country.

One of her speeches was listened to by Mr Nugent Harris, secretary of the Agricultural Organisation Society, (who was the English equivalent of Erland Lee in Canada) who could see the potential for an organisation of farmers' wives who could feel free to speak out without the intimidating presence of their husbands. More than that, they could increase the food production of the country and so could be worthy of financial support.

He was authorised by his board to engage Mrs Watt as an organiser. Madge was charged with opening WIs where ever she could in the UK.

The first one was opened in Anglesey in LlanfairPG, following a big conference at Bangor. Colonel Richard Stapleton-Cotton (Chairman of the North Wales Branch of the A.O.S) heard Madge speak at Bangor and invited her to speak at his own village, which was LlanfairPG. At that meeting, it was unanimously agreed to set up a WI in their village. The rest, as they say, is history. Colonel Cotton felt that if a WI could be established in Wales with its strong church/chapel division it could be set up anywhere. It met in a hall lent by the Marquis and Marchioness of Anglesey, who later lent them money to build their own hall. It met on 11th September 1915.

Madge, with the group, established the basic principles of WI meetings. An institute is not ruled: it rules itself. Self-determination and democracy were not concepts familiar to women in 1915. The motto of the institute should be: 'Help one another,' and the first resolution of the first WI in Great Britain was: 'We, the members of the Llanfair WI, pledge ourselves to do our utmost to make the Institute the centre of good in our neighbourhood.' Three more WIs were opened in Wales – Criccieth, Trefnant and Cefn Institutes before any opened in England.

Six months after the opening of the WIs in Wales, Colonel Cotton wrote a letter to Madge saying that he had been 'one of the many who doubted the capacity of women to conduct even their ordinary business with success but I have learned more about women than I have learned in forty years... I see and believe that women can and will bring all classes, all denominations, all interests, all schools of the best sort together in that common brotherhood of love .... which every man and every women longs for in his or her innermost heart.'

The first WIs in England were set up, again with Madge's guidance, at Singleton in West Sussex and Wallisdown in Dorset.

By the end of the year 1915 in addition to the four in Wales there were two in Kent, three in Dorset and one in Sussex – that is ten in three months. They were spreading like wild fire. Within three years Madge helped bring a hundred WIs into existence.

They were springing up so quickly that the staff at NFWI could not keep up with getting them all established. Madge was deputed to set up a training course for what became known as Voluntary County Organisers: women who would be based at their County HQ and would go out to any groups wanting to become WIs and help them set up their Institute.

The first of these was organised in 1918 by Madge and caused enormous interest. Detailed notes on the speeches and activities at this first training course organised by Madge for the WI were printed in 1918 by the Sussex Federation and they make fascinating reading.

Madge had already decided that, in addition to lectures in the mornings, the afternoons and evenings should be devoted to looking at work in the field, that is, visiting actual WIs in order to learn from them. For this, she needed to base her course in a county which had already got flourishing groups 'on the right lines'.

She selected Sussex and Burgess Hill WI as the focal point. She was incredibly fortunate in that the owners of a 'charming house with large rooms' a Mr and Mrs Bridge, (the local WI President and her husband) lent her their country house, Wyberlye, for the three weeks of the course. This was a beautiful house set in wonderful grounds and although the members of the course were housed in near-by WI members' homes and driven in by car every day, they experienced each day the thrill of learning in a civilised and attractive setting. The drawing room at Wyberlye looks exactly like the drawing room at Denman – only more cluttered! This was Madge's first attempt at a 'mini – Denman' and gave all participants some idea of what owning their own residential college would be like. When Denman opened in 1948 their first courses, like Madge's, ran from Monday to Friday.

Madge recognised that setting the tone was crucial to success. She wrote:

'One felt, too, that it must all be very informal with plenty of time for discussion and questions and that from first to last there must be nothing of set forms of instruction and examination. But yet there had to be both .... I had to be instructing and examining .... But how to do this without obvious effort or making people nervous or introducing a pedantic spirit was rather a problem.

'To meet this desire, I first planned that those who were instructing should also be pupils: that there should be something in which I and the other instructors were learners and that each of those who came to learn should teach the rest of us. I think that perhaps gave the delightful feeling of mix-up which prevented any of us from feeling that we were in any way superior beings.'

Finally, says Madge, 'It was always in my mind that the course must be at once practical and yet stimulating; in short I wished the school to be, as indeed in proved to be, less of a school than an awakening.' It certainly was that.

Twenty three ladies took the course and Madge's report says:

'The following ladies in England have fulfilled part of my requirements, and are able and willing to fulfil the rest, and are therefore to be recommended as WI Organisers'

I love that 'fulfilled part of my requirements:' she set incredibly high standards, but for herself first, then the people she was coaching. Lil Nugent Harris said of her, 'You'd have to be born in heaven to come up to her standard.' Some found her too strict and too direct. But she worked at what she knew to be right and never gave up.

The school covered three weeks. Each week could be taken separately but was designed to build up over the period.

There were sessions on the history of the movement, on the aims, objects and ideals of WIs, on the techniques of running a meeting and running a committee, and organising programmes of activities.

Mrs Clowes, an organiser teaching with Madge, in talking about 'How to Present Aims and Objectives to a Village Audience' says:

'I always tell them, in getting out a programme, to remember three points:

Something to hear
Something to see
Something to do.

This proves of interest for everyone. I explain the glorious unity of the Women's Institute organisation and how the home is the beginning of all that the country will be.'

The final session of each week was a talk on public speaking. This was given by a Miss Peacock who emphasised the need to project the voice without shouting, and the importance of pausing during a speech for emphasis.

Typically, Madge offered herself as a 'horrible example' of speaking and 'had the pleasure of hearing a very candid criticism of faults in delivery and so forth. Then all present were criticised briefly and received useful hints.'

VCOs, now known as WI Advisers, have gone from strength to strength and as well as helping new groups form, they are still today responsible for training days in public speaking.

Like most of these pioneering leaders, Madge belonged to a number of women's organisations including the International Council of Women. During 1919 once the WIs were up and running in Britain and the first VCOs trained, Madge returned to Canada but not before she had 'the satisfaction of starting a WI at Sandringham, with HM the Queen as President.' Madge talked of setting up an international organisation of rural women and tried to persuade everyone to back this scheme.

It took her fourteen years but eventually in 1933 the Associated Country Women of the World was launched at a conference in Stockholm. The famous photo showing this start, shows Madge standing beside a blackboard with the name of the organisation written in English, French, German and Swedish. And of course the NFWI is still today linked with the ACWW. It is only the high cost of travel that discourages British members travelling abroad to wherever the ACWW Conference is.

Madge was its first President and stayed until she retired in 1947. She travelled round the world and visited WIs in many countries.

Although Madge's first job had been a writer, she never wrote her own story. She lived on very little money and moved from one set of rented rooms to another.

During the second world war Madge lived in Victoria, British Columbia and then with her son Sholto in Montreal where she died in 1948.

Madge was a genuine pioneer who moved from one WI in Canada to many more, then brought them to England, creating hundreds more, then finally creating virtually a world-wide web of women.

She knew that women could help build a better world. She had a vision of women coming together in their own villages and working on common goals with shared visions.

She was a builder who believed in the power of women working together, regardless of race, religion or nationality. She believed in women's rights to access to higher education, to careers and opportunities to become individuals by using their skills and talents. And she helped women do this without upsetting their family grouping or breaking up relationships.

Trudie Pearson – Lady Denman

(1884 – 1954)

Trudie Pearson was the little girl who had everything: a rich father, a loving family, ponies, an imposing house in London and an impressive country estate. She grew up to be the young woman who had everything: horses, money, independence and a suitor who was a baron.

What more could a girl ask for?

In Trudie's case – a lot.

She was born to a wealthy engineering contractor, Weetman Pearson and his wife Annie. They were both from Yorkshire and made a striking pair. Annie was the equal of her husband in determination and force of character. Her determination to succeed in society drove Annie to push all her children to advance themselves as far as they could. Despite this, she and her husband were Liberals, both convinced feminists, and determined to do all they could to improve conditions for the poor and needy.

Trudie hated all the dressing up and socialising – the endless dinner parties with the inane chatter. But Trudie could not avoid the country house parties and balls that her mother took her to. Annie was determined that Trudie should marry well – not necessarily a rich man, as they were wealthy themselves, but someone with a title and a future. In 1902, at a ball, when she was 18, Trudie saw at the top of a grand staircase standing on crutches a young officer back from the South African war. He was a young Liberal Peer, the 28 year old Baron Denman. It was not exactly love at first sight, but then given the advantages of each to the other, love might follow. And if it did not, at least there would be a solid match and the joy of children.

Denman courted Trudie assiduously and she went along with this, as he was amusing and a good companion. But when he proposed to her, she was startled and rejected him. She wrote,

'I never thought you were serious till the dance last Friday. I thought we were very good friends and rather amused each other and that was all. I am afraid I was very stupid not to understand. I am sure you will meet lots of people better than I, so please don't be downcast by what I fear is my hardness of heart. I hope this doesn't stop my being always your friend, Trudie Pearson.'

But neither Denman nor Annie were discouraged by this, and Denman kept on until finally Trudie said yes.

Later in her life Trudie gave advice to her daughter:

'Never get married unless you are certain that you would be *absolutely miserable* if you said No. That is the best way a girl can test whether she is in love or only thinks she may be.'

Her first baby was born in 1905 – Thomas. Both mother and baby had severe measles and nearly died.

In the same year, Trudie's father bought her her own country estate, Balcombe in Sussex. Trudie, passionate about hunting, was at first disappointed that Balcombe was not in recognised 'hunting' country, but later appreciated the beauty and unspoilt countryside and its nearness to London.

Denman's ill health dogged the marriage – in summer hay fever and in winter bronchitis meant he frequently had to go away on sea voyages and to the South of France.

Trudie was lonely. A second child was born - a daughter, Judith.

In 1908, Trudie got involved in her first public work. She was elected to the executive of the Women's Liberal Federation. (Her mother was on the committee.) The chairman was the formidable Lady Carlisle – a passionate Temperance supporter – popularly believed to have poured the whole contents of the Castle Howard wine cellars down the drain! This was a powerful organisation pressing for women to be given the vote, led by very strong women. Trudie learned how to handle difficult people and shape agendas so that things were decided on and then acted on. She learned how to speak, how to conquer her shyness, and what the battle for equality with men was like. All these would stand her in good stead later on in life.

The next challenge was Australia. In 1910, Denman was invited to become Governor-General of Australia. This was a great honour, but it also involved a huge expenditure which he would have to meet himself. Denman was only able to accept because Trudie's father provided thousands of pounds.

Trudie liked the challenge of a new country and new responsibilities, but hated all the ceremony involved, the dressing up and socialising and being polite to everyone. She looked for ways of escaping from the daily rituals and found it by riding off as often as she could in trousers into the out-back and living rough for a few days at a time.

Australia was a tough challenge for an unhealthy man and his 26 year old wife with two small children. The Australians were ultra-democratic where every man thought he was twice as good as the next man, and they resented any interference from the old country.

Despite this macho attitude, Trudie found herself being treated as royalty, and severely restricted in what she could do or where she could go. She wrote:

'I am so grand that I am not allowed to go to any but epoch making functions of a national character .... I am also too grand to go into a shop. Can you wonder that most of the Governors' wives are bored to tears?'

She never showed her boredom in public, but tried to present a friendly and sincere character. The press warmed to her: 'Lady Denman is a pleasant-looking lady whom no-one would accuse of beauty until she smiles. Her smile is a miracle, a whole wealth of kind-heartedness and good nature.' And again:

'She does not adopt that pose of haughty disdain which has been so characteristic of some vice-regal ladies in the past. Besides, she smiles.'

Her experience with the Women's Liberal Federation in England in fighting for the franchise gave her a special interest in women's organisations in Australia, where women for nine years had been able to vote in State and Federal Parliaments. When she spoke at a women's meeting in Melbourne, she was able to say:

'This is the first gathering of women I have met who have the vote.'

Closest to her heart was Bush Nursing – a service for women and their families living in remote areas with no access to doctors or hospitals who had to struggle as well as they could with illness or child birth. The idea was to appoint a trained nurse for each area who would cope with emergencies. The famous singer, Dame Nellie Melba, gave a benefit concert which raised £10,000 for an endowment fund. From only one nurse who was in post when Trudie arrived in Australia, the postings grew to twenty by the time she left Australia, and shortly after the First World War there were 47 centres.

At first, the only means of transport was on horseback. There were no ambulances and operations had to be performed in the patient's own primitive home. Later, of course, ambulances and hospitals arrived, plus the famous flying doctor service which flew doctors to an emergency.

Though not an actress herself, Trudie was a great supporter of drama and nearly created the first National Theatre in the Empire. She helped the Melbourne Repertory Theatre Club, and stimulated the project to build a Memorial Theatre to commemorate the 300th anniversary of Shakespeare's death in 1616. Unfortunately, this project was killed off by the war.

In 1913 Trudie had the honour of naming the new capital city of Australia. The name was kept secret until Trudie announced it. No one was sure how to pronounce it. As the card was handed to her, without hesitation Trudie said, 'I name the capital of Australia Canberra' with the emphasis on the first syllable.

Denman's health would not let him stay for the full term and they set out to come home.

They were on board ship when they heard the news of the murder of the Austrian Archduke at Sarajevo and they arrived in Britain just before war was declared.

Denman instantly shot off to join his regiment, while Trudie set up a war charity called 'Smokes for wounded Soldiers' and Sailors' Society (the S.S.S.) She turned her ballroom into a packing room and they supplied all hospital ships and trains and all service hospitals with free smokes. By the time she resigned in 1917, 265 million cigarettes had been supplied, as well as tobacco, pipes and cigars.

As a very heavy smoker herself, she realised how vital cigarettes were to soldiers and sailors under stressful conditions.

Her next venture, with her old friend Nellie Grant, was to make maximum use of waste scraps of food by encouraging all households to keep poultry in the back-yard. They persuaded a friend to design a model back-yard hen-house which they advertised and sold.

But later that year, Trudie was drawn into the movement which would dominate the rest of her life – the WI.

The growth in WI's in war-time was staggering.

From the first WI in Llanfair in September 1915 to autumn 1916, the number had grown to 24. It was felt that a National chairman was needed – Lady Salisbury was invited but declined, so Lady Denman was asked – and she said yes.

The war had produced a desperate need to grow more food. The Minister for Agriculture said, 'England is like a beleaguered city.' There was only about three week's food supply in the country. Trudie insisted that organising the WIs was one excellent way of encouraging the growing of more vegetables, aided later by the development of the Women's Land Army – also led by Trudie.

Alongside the urgency of producing more food was the overwhelming realisation that the institutes could satisfy a permanent need in the lives of country women, whose needs had been for so long ignored by press and Parliament.

The AGM in 1918 – the second in its history – saw the decision taken to change the wording in the constitution from 'non-political' to 'non-party' in recognition of the fact that most things they were striving for required political action, and they urgently needed to discuss and to resolve in order that living conditions could be improved.

After the war, the continued growth in the number of institutes was breath-taking. At the end of 1918, there were 760 institutes; by the start of 1928 they were 4,000; by 1938, there were 5,500 with a total membership of more than 350,000.

There is no doubt that the resolutions passed by successive AGMs of the WI and the repeated discussions and letters to the press, MPs and government ministers have been hugely instrumental in improving conditions in the countryside, and better medical and nursing services. And the woman who led the NFWI for 30 years from 1916 to 1946 with inspiration and unflagging enthusiasm was Trudie. She was there at the end of the first world war and she was still there at the end of the second world war.

From the start, Trudie had encouraged every member to practise active democracy. If democracy meant anything, it meant that as well as claiming the rights to self-determination and self-governance, it involved taking responsibility for some aspect of her institute's work.

In 1937 Trudie made a speech to the AGM, which she later repeated in a broadcast speech to the 350,000 members. She said,

'To my mind the greatest achievement of the Institutes is that we have learned to govern ourselves. We do not believe in dictators; we believe that each member should be responsible for her Institute and should have a share in the work. It may be as a member of Committee; it may be as one of those responsible for the entertainment; it may be as a helper at tea; or as a steward arranging the meeting; but the many jobs that have to be done in the perfect Women's Institute are shared by the members and are not undertaken by one or two super-women. In our movement we enjoy liberty and democratic government. The smallest of the WIs can move a resolution at this great meeting, and if that resolution is carried it becomes the policy of us all.'

Trudie encouraged every individual institute to write to their own MP plus any government ministers. When she went to the House of Commons to talk to a group of members, she saw that every MP was carrying a large bunch of letters. She said,

'One MP suggested that he would have been saved a lot of work if he had received one letter from the County Federation rather than 50 from individual institutes. I suggested, in reply, that it was always possible for one letter to be overlooked, whereas 50 were bound to receive attention. Judging by the way I was greeted and by a chorus of 'Hear, Hears' and laughter, the MPs entirely agreed that there is strength in a united attack.'

Trudie's speeches at successive AGMs in the 1930's urged members to bring pressure to bear on their local councils to improve: piped water supplies to village homes, telephone boxes in villages, electricity for rural areas, proper collection and destruction of refuse, the preserving of the beauty of the countryside and its old buildings, footpaths and the banning of litter.

She was fully aware of the cultural side of the WI movement. At the AGM in 1937, she said,

'Foremost, Women's Institutes have, I think, added to the happiness of country women. Through the Institutes the love of acting, of dancing, of singing and of craft work has been aroused and given opportunity of expression.'

She was keen to promote creative abilities among the members, even to the extent of proposing a competition for an institute song. She wrote,

'When the National Federation was very young, it seemed to some of us that a competition for an Institute song might produce a good but unknown poetess. Miss Hadow took the view that poetry written for a special purpose was unlikely to be good – but still I hoped. Eventually a verse arrived which started with the line 'We are a band of earnest women.' This was too much for me and, as usual, I realised how right Miss Hadow was – hence *Jerusalem* became and remains the WI song.'

The second main interest in Trudie's public life was her chairmanship of the Family Planning Association. She was its first chairman, as she was for the WI, and it was the only chairmanship she insisted on keeping when ill-health forced her to give up all her other work.

She believed so strongly in the need for this organisation – which gave information and help on the various contraceptives available to women – because she believed in marriage as a partnership of equals, which meant that the couple needed to control their fertility and only have a child when both of them really wanted that. This meant that a lot of women had to take charge of contraception and not be left at the mercy of loving, but selfish, husbands.

The issue had been in the news since 1875, when Charles Bradlaugh MP and Mrs Annie Besant, a well-known reformer, decided to republish a book first printed in 1833, which suggested the use of contraceptives as the only way to harmonise mankind's two strongest needs: food and sexual gratification.

They were both prosecuted and found guilty of:

'Unlawfully and wickedly devising, contriving, and intending, as much as in them lay, to vitiate and corrupt the morals as well of youth as of divers other subjects of the queen, and to incite and encourage the said subjects to indecent, obscene, unnatural and immoral practices, and bring them to a state of wickedness, lewdness and debauchery.'

They were sentenced to prison, though Bradlaugh managed to get the conviction quashed on appeal, but the public outrage was enormous.

The Roman Catholic Church banned all discussion and use of contraceptives, and the Church of England initially condemned all practices outright – at their Lambeth Conference in 1918, although later they said it might be allowed in certain circumstances.

This was a tricky situation for Trudie, as many members of the WI were devout Catholics or members of the Church of England, and Trudie feared that they might be appalled if they realised that their WI chairman was at the same time the chairman of the Family Planning Association. But she had seen so many heart-breaking situations of poor women, both in England and Australia who could not keep up, financially or health-wise, with the constant production of infants.

And this was not just a problem for working-class women. Mrs Gladstone was in constant worry over the health of her sister, Lady Lyttleton, who had 7 children in 9 years and then went on to have 4 more. Her doctor warned her that if she conceived a 12th child both mother and child would die. A few months later she became pregnant, and later died in her sister's arms, after giving birth to her 12th child.

Trudie threw all her energies into establishing this movement as a moral force for good, and fought against all the prejudice which it attracted. She later said that this was the most difficult task she had ever undertaken. After her death, the Family Planning Association set up a Memorial in the form of Lady Denman Memorial Clinics. The linking of her name with the clinics gave country women confidence in their services: They fulfil Trudie's special wish that family planning should be available to country women as well as townswomen.

These two organisations – the WI and the Family Planning Association which Trudie chaired for most of her life – although at first may seem to have little in common, in fact are two sides of the same coin. They are both furthering the empowerment of women – encouraging women to take control of their own lives. In an increasingly unstable world, with job security no longer assured, wars, famine and disease rocking third world countries, it is ever more necessary to take control of what we can. Control of fertility is one of the powers that women can exercise, and for the sake of their family and their own health, they should make use of this control. In addition, trying to influence their surroundings – their home, their children's schooling, their working conditions, what they do or can do in any leisure time they have, are all part of building a fulfilling life.

And creating a satisfying rich life for their own family and their community – large or small – is what the WI is all about.

And that is precisely what Trudie Denman was about – all her life.

Standing up for what she felt was right, and fighting apathy and distrust was Trudie's mission in life.

But she did all this while always maintaining a great sense of fun, and an infectious sense of humour. A newspaper report of one of the AGMs gave this picture of the woman who led the meeting:

'She was splendid. She never faltered. She cut short a few of the more verbose and kept others to the point; but she was always ready to help on the more modest, encourage the expression of views, deal swiftly and certainly with a few difficult points of order that arose. She held the whole meeting in her hand, yet never once abused her remarkable influence upon a gathering collected from every corner of England and Wales. By the end of the day she seemed the personal friend of everybody present.'

In her memorial service at Balcombe Parish Church, the Bishop of Chichester, Dr Bell, paid this tribute:

'In her public life there was one great motive by which her work was directed – the determination to do everything she could to help the women of her country. She sought, so far as it lay in her power, to prevent them being trampled upon. She was resolved to secure that, with the help of a sound education and in other ways, they should have every opportunity for the development of their gifts, and for making their full contribution to the life of the community as citizens and country women, as wives and mothers. Lady Denman had a profound belief in the principles of democracy. She trained herself, and (it may be truthfully said) to a considerable extent educated herself, in the practice of these principles when she was quite a young woman, and held them to the end.... To the end of her life she was valiant for the truth which she saw, and set an example in her human love, her service to others and her concern for justice, from which all who knew and loved her may profit.'

Grace Hadow

(1875 – 1940)

Grace Hadow was born on 9th December 1875, at South Cerney, near Cirencester. Her father was the local vicar from a family of vicars. This guaranteed Grace from the start access to a vast range of books – not all religious. Before the days of public libraries and cheap books, vicars held a monopoly on learning in their own parish. And every vicar had an impressive library of books. So Grace, like Jane Austen and the Bronte sisters who were also the daughters of vicars, had access not only to the world of books, but also to the mind of the most literate and best-educated man in the village. It is no surprise that literature became Grace's passion – as with Jane Austen and the Brontes.

Across the road from her father's church was an extraordinary building - called 'the college'. This was not an actual college but a set of 12 residences for the widows and unmarried daughters of clergy from the surrounding dioceses. This institution was a huge benefit to the ladies who lived there and they in turn contributed some skills in music, crafts, literature and philosophy to the village, which was made up of farmers, craftsmen and labourers.

One set of elderly ladies struck awe into Grace and her brothers and sisters by getting up at 5 o'clock every morning to study Greek. Could this be the start of Grace's determination to do well herself academically, but also to open the doors to other women, of whatever age, to study Greek or any other subject they wanted?

Grace's imagination was fed with legend and folk-lore, and she never lost this interest in later life, as she felt it helped make links between people living in the past and ourselves today, because the stories are handed down through the generations.

From her mother Grace inherited quickness and a sense of fun, and a love of language. When she was told off for asking for things at tea time Grace muttered, 'I am staring at that cake.'

Her mother always said 'I used to put food and education first,' when she discussed the difficulties of coping. 'Other things such as clothes do not matter.'

Following up this policy Grace's mother sent her to private tutors and a private school.

Truro High School in Cornwall followed and then three glorious years at Oxford University, where the world opened out for Grace. She was a brilliant literature scholar who got a first class degree in English. She did a stint in America, teaching at Bryn Mawr for a year then back to Oxford where she taught English. She saw literature as the best way to increase understanding of human nature, of character and of relationships, domestic, national and international.

Her first love was drama – Shakespeare and the Elizabethans – 'So close to life, and so rich in imagination and in lyric song with music.' She was attracted to the medieval period and Chaucer, whom she felt was the essence of England. She loved Milton, George Herbert, Traherne, Wordsworth and Dickens.

She put on the medieval play 'Everyman' and played Everyman herself. 'None who saw this performance could fail to be moved by it, perfectly simple – unpretentious as it was,' wrote L C Kempson. 'But all who took part in it seemed to be living again in spirit the 'heart-breaking realities of Everyman' when, the play being over, actors and audience mingled in the Summerville garden in the prosaic business of tea and talk, those who had taken part in the play experienced the curious sensation of leaving a world of reality to enter a world that was artificial. In the brief span representing the pilgrimage of Everyman 'into the heavenly sphere' the eternal truths had manifested themselves in the simple symbolism of the old play, and something of Grace Hadow's own spiritual quality had entered into that symbolism and clothed it with life.'

Grace's elder brother was Henry Hadow (1859 – 1937), who was also her godfather – he was sixteen years older than she was.

English scholar, educationist, critic and music historian, he was a Fellow and Dean of Worcester College. Both he and Grace were tall and elegant and distinguished looking.

For a wonderful few years, they both lectured at two different Oxford colleges but shared meals, social visits, trips to the theatre and their beloved music concerts. They shared wide reading, deep thinking, quick, perceptive brains and a delicious sense of wit and humour. They collaborated on the Oxford Treasury of English Literature, while Henry wrote books on music and edited the Oxford History of Music.

Grace missed Henry enormously when he left Oxford to be Principal of Armstrong College, Newcastle in 1909. A pillar of her life was removed from regular daily contact.

She would probably have stayed teaching at Oxford for life if her father had not died and her mother become ill. In answer to those who said she should not give up her career to look after her mother, she said: 'There is always someone else who can do other things equally well, but no one else can do this particular thing.' She moved between occasional teaching in Oxford and almost full-time care for her mother in Cirencester. Living in Cirencester, as opposed to the gorgeous 'other world' of Oxford, brought her into contact with ordinary people, many of whom were without the basics of life and inarticulate into the bargain. She joined the cause for women's suffrage – starting a branch in Cirencester.

She was writing more than ever before: she did a book on *Chaucer and his times* for the Home University Library in 1914. He was one of her great passions. She appreciated particularly his ever present sense of humour. She said:

'Humour is the faculty which enables us to love while we laugh and to love the better for laughter.'

She wrote articles or booklets on subjects which interested her and wrote many articles anonymously for the WI.

When war came in 1914, she immersed herself in local war-work. She helped house and look after refugees from Belgium and heard harrowing tales of their cruel treatment by the Germans; to English soldiers billeted around her she taught French, as a preparation for going to France to fight. She took a passionate interest in the situation of English women doctors, who were rejected by the British authorities but welcomed by the French, where their surgery helped many troops. She encouraged women to band together to cultivate the gardens of men serving at the front or to run cooperative poultry farms.

In 1916 she says, 'I've just been elected a member of the Gloucestershire Chamber of Agriculture. A very odd effect of the war on an Oxford teacher of English literature.'

Mrs Hadow's diary records: 'July 10th 1916: the Women's Institute established. Grace President and chief speaker.'

Later on Grace reports:

'We have founded 17 WIs in surrounding villages.'

In spring 1917 her mother died, which was devastating for Grace. She sold the family home in Cirencester and went to London to get a job to help full-time with the war effort. To every one's amazement, including hers, she was offered a job as director of a subsection of the Ministry of Munitions. This turned out to be what would now be called 'H.R.' She was not required to make bombs or shells: she was put in charge of the welfare of women workers – their health and happiness outside working hours.

This involved: lodgings for workers, their houses, transport, crèches, maternity homes and clubs. It set the foundations for important moves forward in social welfare later on.

She organised a residential conference at Lady Margaret Hall in Oxford in the summer of 1918. She needed no persuasion to understand the value of getting people away from their desks and homes in order to concentrate on better understanding of, and communication between, different subsections of her department.

She gave lectures up and down the country including talking on her own subject – literature. She gave a talk on Nature Poetry to five hundred munition workers, men and women on a Friday night and to her amazement never had a more responsive audience. She said:

'They were quite a rough type and my heart was in my boots when I began, especially as I had been told the employer's point of view which was that no sane person could expect factory hands to listen to stuff like that. And they came to such an extent that there was no standing room. How's that for a working man and woman after a hard day's work?'

Doing her job looking after the women workers in war time had stretched her abilities deliciously – possibly the most fulfilling job she had done to date. She now needed something similar in peace time. She wanted to take part in building a better Britain. Work in munitions had shown her the value of social services, and she knew that the future lay in developing education for adults as a means of developing responsible citizens – Barnett House in Oxford offered her this opportunity. And it could be what she wanted it to be.

It would be a centre for information on social and economic issues, for talks and lectures, and it would provide a library of books. Amazingly Oxford County Council had refused the offer of a Carnegie grant for starting a county library that would ultimately be paid for from the rates, because they were convinced that 'Oxfordshire people don't want to read.' Grace was determined to provide books so that people had the opportunity to learn.

Later she became Principal to the Society of Oxford Home Students which made it possible for students living at home in Oxford to attend lectures in the University. This later became St Anne's College.

In 1919 she was elected to the NFWI Executive and became Vice-Chairman to Lady Denman – a job Grace held until she died in 1940.

'Grace identified herself with the movement till it became part of her,' wrote Helena Deneke, her close colleague and biographer. 'She brought to the movement her intellect, her experience, her training and her gifts.'

Lady Denman recalls her first meeting with her:

'I remember how her quickness in seeing the essential point of whatever was being discussed, and her most entertaining comments made those early committee meetings stimulating and interesting. Miss Hadow's history was not known to me then, and I confess I was startled when I discovered her academic record. I could not believe that anyone of Miss Hadow's knowledge could give such serious consideration to the views of anyone as ignorant as myself. I never really got used to Miss Hadow's humility of mind, and during the long years of our association I was impressed by the way she received suggestions from us all.'

And isn't that precisely the point of a democratic organisation like the WI? Grace wrote the preface to the first edition of the Handbook of the NFWI published in 1921:

'As a nation we are learning to think for ourselves ....; we go about with a perpetual 'why?' in our minds if not on our lips 'Why should these things be? And on the answer to that 'why?' depends the fate of our country, for it involves the meaning of democracy. Democracy is not a game of grab, an attempt on the part of each individual to push to the front; its ideal is that of mutual service, of public duty as a matter of course .... The true democrat resembles Chaucer's Clerk of Oxford, of whom it is recorded that

'Gladly would he teach and gladly learn.'

That exactly expresses the institute ideal:

All women of the village, rich and poor, gentle and simple, learned and unlearned, come together with the one idea of helping each other. All pay the same subscription, have the same rights, the same privileges, the same responsibilities. Each contributes what she has to the common store .... 'If you know a good thing, pass it on,' is one of the principles of the institute movement, and the result is a common bond of fellowship which unites first the women of one village and then the women of the county and then the country.

'.............. Interest in our home leads naturally and inevitably to questions of housing, sanitation, infant welfare and kindred topics. The members learn to realise their responsibilities towards the community in which they live, and from an interest in their own village and their own county, come to see the connection between their affairs and those of the nation at large. It would be difficult to plan a better training for the exercise of the vote – a training entirely free from all party and sectarian bias.

'Without the war it might have been difficult to induce women of all classes to meet together, but the war ,made this seem natural and simple – as indeed it is – and the spirit which it implies goes far beyond the mere details of cooking and mending: it is the basis of citizenship.'

Almost at the start of the NFWI in Britain, Grace is emphasising citizenship as being at the heart of the movement, underlining what was first said by Addie and Madge. She had an unerring instinct for quality in literature and music. She wrote a letter to Home and Country in December 1923.

'I have recently been at Exhibitions or Council Meetings at which the whole assembly has joined in singing Sir Hubert Parry's setting of Blake's Jerusalem. Many WI members have said how much they would like to sing it at our Annual Meeting in London, and I write to urge that WIs or County Federations which approve of this suggestion might write to Headquarters and ask if this could be arranged.

'It should be clearly understood that when a WI makes this request, it pledges itself to learn words and tune by heart. The attempt cannot be a success unless every delegate is ready to sing whether she thinks she can sing or whether she thinks she cannot. Both words and music are simple and dignified and easy to learn. Incidentally the learning would give pleasure to any WI and would afford an excellent opportunity for a short talk either on Blake's poetry, or on poems about England. We have looked in vain for a national 'Institute Song'. Here is one made to our hand and one which some counties have already adopted.

Yours truly
Grace E Hadow'

Just as important as citizenship is personal development. Grace said:

'As institutes developed, increasing attention was paid to educational facilities .... in instance after instance it was found to be true that women whose natural abilities were starving began to discover their power of organisation, their skill in handicrafts, their innate sense of beauty.'

One example was recorded by Grace:

'A few weeks ago I was chatting to a woman obviously very poor and hard worked,

'Do you like poetry?' I asked, and her face lit up.

'What I'd like,' she said, 'would be to recite, if only someone would tell me how to say words.' I asked her if she had ever acted. 'Only in a pageant,' she answered and said softly to herself, 'I'll never forget the colour of that.'''

Grace believed passionately that cultural subjects were open to all men and women and you only had to reach out to make them yours. Helena Deneke again:

'Grace found tongue for what institutes stand for by living it; and in this way the movement became bone of her bone, and flesh of her flesh.'

She died in 1940 as she was entering the second year of her presidency of the Oxfordshire Federation of WIs. Her county federation committee said of her:

'It is difficult to believe that we shall not see Miss Hadow again. She was so full of life, so full of gaiety, and we counted on her as one counts on air, or water, or sunshine .... One of the rarest and most brilliant women of England was ours. She gave us her fine intellect, her wit, her courage and her humour, and we enjoyed them and loved them for they were ruled by her loving kindness.'

Isn't that the most wonderful thing – that this brilliant woman was *ours.* Just as Grace as a child had access to her father's books and to his educated mind, so the members of the WI had access for many years to the learning, wit and love of Grace Hadow.

Elizabeth Irving – Lady Brunner

(1904 – 2003)

Theatre comes to the WI: enter Elizabeth Irving.

Elizabeth Irving was part of a theatrical dynasty – theatre was in her blood. Her grandfather was Sir Henry Irving the famous actor who filled the enormous Lyceum Theatre in London nightly with people agog to hear him and Ellen Terry playing Shakespeare. Her father was the elder son of Sir Henry and like his father was an actor – manager. Her mother, Dorothea Baird, became famous overnight when she created the part of Trilby in the play based on the novel by Gerald Du Maurier, and her brother was a well-known stage designer.

When she was born, her father chose the names for her: Dorothea (after her mother) which means 'gift of God' in Greek and Elizabeth, which means 'gift of God' in Hebrew. To both her parents she was always a gift from God. And later she was very much so to the WI.

She first appeared on the stage in 1916 when she was 12 at the Savoy Theatre in London, walking on with the guests in the wedding scene in 'The Bells'. Her father played Matthias, the part made famous by her grandfather. She said, 'I think I had to say three words: "Good morning Burgomaster."'

The only two women in the audience at her debut were her mother, Dorothea Baird, and Violet the wife of the dramatist Ben Travers. Ben later became Elizabeth's greatest friend.

At the age of 16 she played Titania in 'A Midsummer Night's Dream' at the Court Theatre in 1920. And the following year she re-created the part her mother had first played – Trilby. She was as talented as she was beautiful. A critic wrote of her performance: 'The charm and beauty of Miss Elizabeth Irving would have been of little avail .... if she had not inherited the histrionic ability of her mother and her father.'

She then played Margrete as a guest actress with the O.U.D.S. in 'The Pretenders' by the great Norwegian dramatist Henrik Ibsen at the New Theatre. Later in 1922 she made a silent film of Charlotte Bronte's 'Shirley' playing the part of Shirley opposite Clive Brook (no copy of the film has unfortunately survived). In February 1924 she played Amy in 'Alice sit-by-the-fire' by J M Barrie at the St James's Theatre.

But later that year she met Felix Brunner, of Brunner, Mond (which later became part of ICI).

After her engagement in 1926, she began her long service as a voluntary worker by joining the House Committee of the Elizabeth Garrett Anderson Hospital. In the same year she married Felix and gave up being a professional actress. Over the next 8 years, she had 5 children – all boys, one of whom, Nicholas, died of meningitis.

In 1937, Felix and Elizabeth bought Grey's Court in Oxfordshire and Elizabeth took control of the house, garden and farm. She was particularly interested in their herd of pedigree Guernsey cows and she used to make butter herself.

She joined the village WI, took part in the movement's response to the Government's request for help with housing city children escaping from the bombing by welcoming two families of evacuees from London. In 1941 she became Chair of the Oxfordshire Federation and later that year she was voted on to the National Executive.

Her garden was not just for growing flowers and shrubs: it was for socialising, for welcoming guests, for hosting village fetes, pageants, plays and musical evenings.

The most notable was a Son et Lumiere drama, directed by Christopher Ede in 1959 and 1961. Robert Gittings wrote the play, which had links with Grey's about the murder of Sir Thomas Overbury in 1613. The pianist Dennis Matthews wrote the music.

A year after retiring as Chair of the NFWI, she led the WI Drama festival: five plays on the lives of poets were commissioned, and she and her son Barnabas played in Robert Gitting's play about William Cowper.

Although she had stopped acting professionally when she married, she still acted in amateur shows and more importantly she carried with her into every other job she did the essence of acting. Contrary to what a lot of people believe, a good actress is not 'pretending' to be someone or to 'feel' some emotion. She is searching for the truth and playing that with complete conviction. So Elizabeth in her public life displayed the marks of a great actress: sincerity, truth and emotional power. And of course a commanding voice.

She gave her finest performance at the AGM in 1945 when she persuaded 6,000 women to vote to set up a WI College.

To an audience doubtful about the value of such an enterprise and worried about the cost and whether they could afford to run such an expensive thing – even Lady Denman had asked at first, 'but would it be used enough?' – a strong case had to be made and it had to be done persuasively. Summoning all her powers as an actress Elizabeth launched into her eight minute speech.

'I want you to imagine a place that will be homely and welcoming, where in the pleasantest possible surroundings, away from responsibility and distractions of our usual lives, we can learn about useful practical crafts, and in addition where we can become better informed about the things going on in the world today, where we can learn more of our heritage, and consider and discuss our future.

'At our College we want to be able to continue the work we have begun in our Institutes. We want to give our members opportunities for learning and thinking, in a less distracting atmosphere than the two and a half hours once a month into which, so optimistically, we crowd our manifold activities.

'At a WI College of our own, we should be free to experiment along our own lines in the kind of course we think would best suit our member's needs. Besides this, there is an undoubted advantage in a group of people joining together for purposes of learning and study, who already have a common background and point of view. This does not by any means imply a narrow outlook or field of vision. Indeed, one of the advantages of a WI College seems to be that, including as we should women of all kinds and ages from the whole of England and Wales, we should have a richer and more diverse common background than would students at a local or regional college.

'Subjects we would wish to include would be ones of general interest and which would create an active interest in citizenship – the future of the village and rural life – local government and education and housing – life in other countries as Lady Denman suggests – history and literature – as well as the more specialist one of music, drama, handicrafts, agriculture, horticulture and the domestic arts. Besides these we should want to have occasional schools and conferences for the study of our own institute affairs.........

'General opinion seems to be that accommodation for 40 to 50 students should be aimed at, housed in and around a traditional country house, with small holding and garden attached, and from which the College could be supplied with farm, garden and dairy produce. There would need to be ample facilities for dramatic and musical activities, such as a large barn which could be converted for the purpose if the house itself did not include a large enough room. The kitchen and service quarters should be planned with great care to afford examples of the best modern domestic equipment, managed with the maximum of efficiency. We would like to see in all bedrooms and living rooms examples of our handicrafts – cotton printing, patch work, quilting, weaving, rug making............

'To sum up. A college centrally situated could become a much-needed home and focus for our movement. It would provide a means of attracting and interesting the incoming younger members, and it would open new vistas to our older ones. It must be able to welcome our most reluctant and diffident members; it must provide them with the sympathy and encouragement that their first approaches will undoubtedly need. It must provide fun and relaxation as well as instruction. It must not be a place where only our most forceful intellectuals vie with each other in solving the world's problems. What we teach must be related to the everyday practical things that make up our members' lives. In addition, there must be inspiration and a vision of wider horizons, so that life and the living of it becomes most important and worthwhile.'

What a climax. And what a result: the motion to have their own college was passed. All they had to do now was to find the right large house and buy it, furnish it, equip it, staff it and then fill it with tutors and students. And of course they did this triumphantly. Many stately homes were bought in the late 1940's mostly by local councils, and turned into adult colleges. Many of these have since closed. But Denman has weathered the economic storms over the past few years.

So Elizabeth's faith in the project was amply rewarded. There is a lovely photo of her with Anne Stamper, the NFWI Archivist, on the lawn in front of Denman in the sunshine. This is on the back cover of Anne's superb book 'Rooms off the Corridor,' NFWI 1998.

Elizabeth was elected Chair of the NFWI in 1951, which coincided with the Festival of Britain. This was a celebration of all things British, including industry, trade, culture and the arts, mounted with colour and flair: an assertion of vitality and enterprise after years of austerity and post-war reconstruction.

This *was* Elizabeth and she rode it, like her namesake on the throne, in triumph. She was beautiful and charismatic and had the ability to talk to anyone in society and to persuade them to do things. Under her Chairmanship, Denman thrived and the whole notion of all members having access to education in all its aspects but particularly in the arts was given enthusiastic leadership by Elizabeth.

She initiated, and for 19 years ran, the Keep Britain Tidy Campaign, and in 1964 was awarded an OBE for her work with this enterprise.

The WI was central to Elizabeth's life. Helen Carey, herself Chairman of the NFWI from 1999 – 2003, said of her,

'The WI was her lasting passion and joy .... of particular interest to her was the cultural life of a community which, she believed, contributed to spiritual well-being. She actively promoted and made available art, music and drama to a wider audience through membership of the WI.'

Elizabeth herself once said, 'I cannot think how you would live in a village if you didn't belong to the WI.'

Ben Travers, the dramatist, who wrote a whole string of farces which were put on at the Aldwich Theatre in London, became close friends with Elizabeth. Through him, she was able to keep in contact with the stage and with actors.

In his auto biography, 'Vale of Laughter,' he wrote a moving tribute to her, and asked an impossible question:

'Elizabeth has always presented a problem: is she more beautiful in looks than she is kind of heart or the other way about? I think the only solution is that it's a dead heat.'

From the man who wrote over 20 plays, 30 screen plays and 5 novels and kept Britain in helpless laughter, this is some tribute.

Ciceley McCall

(1900 – 2003)

Cicely literally spanned the whole of the 20th Century. She was born in 1900 and died in 2003.

Cicely's life story is rich and varied. It sometimes reads like a Hollywood movie, and sometimes like the starkest drama you have ever seen. Throughout it, whether she is with princes and princesses, prostitutes, girls on remand, mental patients or members of the WI, Cicely displays a concern which is always practical and always positive.

She nearly never started her life at all. When she was 4, she developed appendicitis. The family were all away from home on holiday in Kent, and the local GP told Cicely's father that the only man who could save her was the famous surgeon Sir Watson Cheyne, who of course lived in London. By one of those fortunate coincidences which happily occurred fairly often in her life, Sir Watson was actually only a few miles away, treating another patient. He came, and operated on Cicely on the dining room table, presumably, said Cicely, with her usual dry sense of humour, after breakfast had been cleared away.

This sums up Cicely's attitude to life: whatever happens, do the best you can with your situation. Like Mr Micawber she is confident 'something will turn up.' Unlike Mr Micawber, though, with Cicely something always does turn up. She is interested in such a range of social problems, and wants to do things all the time – make her contribution to society not by talking but by putting in action her ideas on how to treat the poor, the mentally ill, the elderly, people on remand, women. She is a feminist and wants equality of opportunity and equality of treatment for women. She is also a socialist and wants the inequalities in society to be levelled out – and this can only be done by political resolve and action. Above all, she is a humanitarian: politics takes you a long way with physical changes. There remains the emotional: how you treat people in your care. Like most of the other pioneers in the WI, Cicely does this with love.

She was the daughter of a successful lawyer who came from Dublin to make his fortune in London. For a time, he was very successful and the family lived in some style. Gradually, however, his work fell away and the family had to rein in their expenditure. Worse still, there would not be money to allow Cicely to live a life of leisure – she would have to work for her living.

She made a good start by passing the entrance exam to St Hugh's College in Oxford, but then fell foul of a stupid regulation: she was one minute late in coming back to her college digs, and the door had been shut and bolted. She was sent down for the rest of the term, and never recovered her composure after that. She failed her degree and realised she had to get a job.

She signed on at a secretarial school and learned shorthand and typing.

Then one of the many lucky things that happened to Cicely happened now. In 1923 she was offered a job in Poland: to teach English to the children of a Prince and Princess. She enjoyed teaching the children and also enjoyed an extravagant life style. When guests were present, which was often, the food was sumptuous. At the same time Cicely, with her social awareness, could see that the servants, the peasants, existed on potatoes and even those were getting scarce.

She was there for nearly two years, then she went to India to keep house for her brother Geoffrey. Again her life was privileged: she visited Agra and Delhi and was waited on by servants. After a year, she felt she should be more serious about life and came back to London.

She got a job as sales girl in a knit wear shop but assessing her chances of promotion as nil, she left and joined the well-known scholastic agency Gabbitas Thring. This paid more money but she still had trouble making ends meet. Again, she left.

She got news of a better paid job – twice what she was getting at Gabbitas Thring - coupled with the sheer excitement of going to Egypt.

There followed three years from 1926 of the most extraordinary encounters that anyone could envisage – especially for a well-brought up young lady from London.

The job was in Cairo with the International Bureau for the Suppression of Traffic in Women and Children. They advertised for someone over 30, who spoke French fluently and who had experience of committee work. Cicely was 26, had no knowledge of committee work, but could speak French. She got the job and ended up working in a shelter for prostitutes run by the Bureau.

When one of the committee members questioned Cicely's usefulness – did no one in London realise the nature of the work she would be doing in Egypt? – the chairman replied in support of Cicely: 'Miss McCall has lots of experience in the life of prostitutes, not like you and I, but as a professional.' That put paid to the questioner, and the anecdote was repeated to Cicely by delighted observers.

The problem was huge. Girls were shipped or kidnapped into brothels from all over Europe. They were hundreds of miles from home in a foreign country with no one to turn to. They were powerless to resist abuse by clients or pimps. There was a half-hearted attempt to 'regulate' the work by licensing prostitutes which never worked, and a pathetic attempt at weekly medical inspections which had no effect either. Cicely gives a graphic description of the farce of these 'inspections'.

It was estimated that 90% of all young male Egyptians had VD. There were 697 licensed prostitutes in Cairo and 808 in Alexandria – with 100s more who were unlicensed. Cicely did her best to reassure the girls and to make sure that they were kept safe and, where possible, sent back to their home country. She offered them protection and support but of course could do nothing to discourage the trade: there were no jobs – or hardly any - for women in Cairo.

Cicely was asked by the London office of the Bureau to write a report on conditions in Egypt, which she did, and the League of Nations published it. Cicely was a brilliant report writer, as was shown later when she worked for the NFWI.

She was next offered a job on a Cairo weekly magazine, The Sphinx, which involved reporting on social functions and visiting celebrities. The first famous person she interviewed was Charlie Chaplin, who turned out to be shy and self-effacing. She later interviewed the famous English actors Sybil

Thorndike and Lewis Casson, who were playing 'St Joan' by Bernard Shaw in Cairo.

While in Cairo, she visited Palestine, Jerusalem, Bethlehem, Galilee and the Black Sea. She went up the Nile and saw Luxor, Abu Simbel and Tutankhamun's Tomb – with the mummy still in it.

A woman friend suggested to her that they should drive across Europe together to get home, she to Innsbruck and Cicely to London.

They set out in Cicely's Morris Cowley, drove to Alexandria, crossed the Mediterranean and on to Constanza in Rumania. On the boat occurred another of the wonderful chance meetings that Cicely seemed to attract: they met Princess Ileana, the daughter of Queen Marie of Rumania. She invited them to come and have tea with her mother, the Queen. They stayed a few days, were treated like royalty and then left to continue their drive across Europe. They went to Budapest and Vienna, then when they got to Oberammergau, the back axle on the car broke. They somehow got it towed to a garage and still made it in time to see the famous passion play.

Back in London a friend suggested Cicely should train as a social worker. So she did.

During her training she visited a range of prisons, including Wandsworth, Holloway, Brixton , Leeds, and several boys' borstals.

She got a job as Assistant House Mistress at the Girls Borstal at Aylesbury, then at Holloway Prison. She tried to get the girls interested in reading and gave them classes each evening. She wrote a book based on these experiences called 'They always come back.' Basically, Cicely is asking 'but need they?'

A spell at Exeter Approved School followed, and it was in Devon where she met Elizabeth Dashwood, otherwise known as E M Delafield, author of 'Diary of a Provincial Lady'. When Cicely had flu followed by a heart attack, it was Elizabeth and her children who looked after her and restored her to health.

And it was through Elizabeth Dashwood that she came to work for the WI. Lady Denman wanted to increase the number of Advisers at Head Office. There were already Advisers for Handicraft and Marketing plus a General Adviser. Lady Denman wanted to introduce an Educational Adviser.

She could see the need to broaden women's interests from just domestic affairs to current affairs, and issues of importance to women. She asked Elizabeth, who was a member of the Board, could she suggest someone suitable to lead the new project and Elizabeth said 'Cicely'. She got the job after a frightening interview with members of the Board, who felt that she was too young – again!

One of her first tasks was to travel through the counties of England and Wales to introduce the idea of adult education to the WI members.

Together with Adeline Vernon, chair of the education subcommittee, she travelled round the counties. The usual routine was to spend one week each month at WI Head Quarters to attend committees and write reports, and three weeks touring the counties. In her 8 years with the WI, she visited every county in England and all but one of the Welsh counties.

She was always made aware of the poverty around the country. She would be put up overnight by a member of the WI – except, she says, in Durham, where so many miners were out of work that it was not possible for their hard-pressed wives to offer hospitality.

Sometime after the start of the War, Cicely thought she should be doing more for the war effort and thought about joining up. She telephoned Lady Denman, who nearly exploded, and told her in no uncertain terms that she was much more valuable where she was, as she was preparing women all over the country for life after the war and that was much more important than joining up and doing some clerical job.

Cicely stayed.

In the 1940's., conditions in many parts of rural England were still deplorable. The WI passed a resolution in 1943 that water supply, electricity and sewerage should become a national responsibility and that local authorities should be compelled to take action to ensure as good a supply in the country as in the towns. To back up this resolution, a questionnaire on available water supplies was sent to every WI in the country and replies were received from 3,500 villages. One of Cicely's responsibilities was to summarise the replies and compile a report. The final report was widely distributed, was quoted in the House of Commons debate and received wide coverage in the Press. It gave a fascinating though horrifying account of living conditions in rural England:

'In most villages few houses had indoor sanitation. There was no piped water, and many villagers had to carry water from a stand pipe more than 200 feet away. Some schools had no water supply at all, and the great majority had "earth closets"'. Some of the details are horrendous:

'In Lindsell in Essex the school earth closets are emptied 3 times a year. Effluent from various cess pits runs into a ditch near the school just to add to the general odour .... At Debenham in East Suffolk women carry their lavatory pails a quarter of a mile to empty them'.

Cicely knew that first only by everyone knowing that these horrific conditions existed, and then determining to change them, would anything be achieved. Her report ensured that all her readers knew about these conditions. What to do next? WI members had to be prepared to pass resolutions, and then learn how to talk powerfully enough to convince doubting politicians to change the regulations, and to supply the money to make this happen.

The NFWI had provided conferences to train members in committee procedures, and now Cicely was instrumental in adding to these by organising speakers' schools. 'If WI members of the future were to play their part in local government they must not only know accepted procedure but they must also be articulate enough to negotiate it effectively'. This is crucial in any democratic organisation. It's no good knowing what you want to say, if you cannot physically stand up and say it. So, encouraging women to speak persuasively has always been part of WI educational programmes, after Cicely had started them.

Towards the end of the war, Cicely began to think she should practise what she had preached to the members and take up an active role in local government. She consulted a friend who said emphatically, 'You should stand for Parliament.' So she gave her name to Labour Party Head Quarters, and was selected as a candidate. Although the date of the next General Election had not been fixed, the NFWI thought that adoption as a candidate would not be compatible with her work, and they sacked her in 1945.

Despite the fact that at this time, Lady Denman was Chair of the Women's Liberals, the Chair of the Organisation Committee was a Labour candidate, and several WI Executive members had a prominent role in their local Conservative Parties, the staff being full time were obviously in a different situation from elected members, and so the Board was probably right to decide that no-one could do two jobs at the same time.

What is harder to understand is why, when Cicely failed to win her first attempt at election, she was not offered her job back at the NFWI.

Once again, Cicely had to look for other work.

Cicely found a job as the first social worker at St Audry's Hospital in Woodbridge and found a horrifying situation. This was an old mental hospital with a thousand beds, and every ward was kept locked. There were no amenities in the hospital, no canteen, no tea-trolley, no visiting library, no freedom for the patients and no pocket money. After Cicely started, to their astonishment the old men got pocket money for smokes and the old ladies for sweets – and that was just the start of a whole liberating regime to humanise what had become a regimented institution.

Cicely had been a prime mover in establishing a WI College after the war. Together with Betty Christmas, Cicely drew up the first blue print. When, finally, a house was bought and the college was opened in 1948 it was named after Lady Denman.

The first principal, called a warden in those days, was Betty Christmas, a bright, forthright woman, determined to prove herself. She had enthusiasm, charm and a welcoming smile – all of which are essential to a principal of this kind of college, where establishing an affirming personal relationship is so important. But, as with all residential adult colleges, there were problems, the main one being the underuse of the college.

WI students arrived on Monday evening and left on Friday morning – making a four day week. No week end courses were offered, and the college closed down for all of August and part of September and for Christmas and Easter. So, for many days and weeks of the year, the buildings and equipment were standing unused.

Betty developed cancer and sadly died.

Cicely got a letter some months after this, asking her to consider taking on the job of warden. She willingly accepted this and started work.

One of her first moves was to start week-end courses to complement the Monday to Friday courses.

There was interest and support in many WIs for their new college, and lots of money was raised by groups all over the country. The problem was that no WI member was allowed to visit Denman to see this wonderful new addition to their resources, except during two weeks in August, when the college was empty.

Cicely was appalled when she was told that even if a WI member was close to the college, on holiday or for any other reason, and called in to see if she could look round, she was literally turned away.

Cicely instantly suggested that any WI member would be welcome at any time to look round, provided they let the college know in advance.

Now, it was the staff's turn to be appalled. 'Who would show them around?' they asked, 'We're all too busy.'

Cicely simply said, 'I will', and that was that. And show them round she did. For at least six months after they started this new scheme, the college was inundated with visitors, but then things quietened down. The value of this scheme, in terms of public relations, cannot be exaggerated, and Cicely was right: it is the job of the principal to cope. You are selling a college and it has to be done right.

Cicely initiated three courses which at the time were considered completely revolutionary: a weekend course for husbands and wives; a three day course for mothers and their babies; and a family weekend. For the married couples' weekend they ran the usual programme of three or four simultaneous courses. For the family weekend they had a reduced choice but provided children's beds, some cots, some tents and a playground in the garden, which was manned by volunteer Marcham WI members, a Guide Captain and other WI supporters.

Things seemed to be going very well until ....

One day in the autumn of 1958, Lady Dyer (the NFWI Chairman) paid the college a visit, and Cicely walked round the gardens with her and showed her the avenue of young red oaks, donated by the Canadian WIs, which the staff had all taken turns in weeding.

'I don't know how you have done so much in such a short time,' said Lady Dyer.

A few weeks later Cicely had a telegram early one morning from a WI Executive member, a personal friend from Norfolk saying, 'All my support and love. Good luck.' She had no idea what it meant but when the post arrived there was a letter from Lady Dyer sacking Cicely for the second time. When asked why, she was told that there was a staff crisis, that her administration was hopeless and that the Executive had decided she must go.

She had 12 days to hand over the office, and three weeks to clear out of the Warden's cottage. After the 12 days she was forbidden to set foot inside the college unless she had written permission from Lady Dyer.

This draconian treatment suggested that she had been found guilty of some serious crime or moral outrage. As Cicely said,

'If I had defrauded the college or been found in bed with the gardener, the terms of my dismissal could hardly have been more insulting. Letters of protest came pouring in from WIs and their supporters, but the decision stood.'

Lady Dyer said that Cicely was 'a square peg in a round hole.' Yet this same administrative failure had halved the college deficit in a year, and doubled the intake of students, thereby enabling the NFWI to apply for an increased grant from the Ministry of Education, which came through the week after she left Denman. The truth was that Cicely had wanted to move too fast for the staff of the college, and the members of the Board and so had to go. But her work had opened up the College for many hundreds of students and made the place more responsive to women's different needs.

Her work led the way to future developments by other principals and helped inspire tutors and students all over Britain.

After Denman, Cicely ended up in Norfolk, and became deeply involved with the Norfolk and Norwich Association for Mental Health, out of which grew the innovative Group Home Scheme – where recovered mental patients lived together with no resident supervision; they were responsible for their own housekeeping, in a shared house in an ordinary street.

Persuading everyone involved was incredibly difficult. First the neighbours who were apprehensive about these peculiar people, and had to be talked to very sensitively by Cicely. Then the patients themselves, who were so used to the institutional regulations and being treated as unable to do anything for themselves, that at first they panicked about having freedom to do things when they wanted to. When they gradually discovered that, for example, they could make a cup of tea for themselves whenever they wanted, their joy became almost unbearable.

The success of the Group Homes led to their being set up in other counties, and other countries. In a kind of pay-back for the WI being brought from Canada to Britain, Cicely was invited to do a tour of Ontario to talk about her Group Homes. Soon after she returned from Canada, a Group Home was opened in Ottawa.

The wheel had come full circle. Inspiration had flowed from Canada to the UK with the creation of the WI and now inspiration was flowing back from the UK to Canada, with the establishing of independent living for recovering mental patients. It's all to do with the empowerment of women in all ways and in all situations. And this is what Cicely McCall did all her life.

Book list

I gratefully acknowledge the help I have received from the following books, which are all highly recommended:

1 The Story of the Women's Institute Movement J W Robertson Scott. The Village Press 1925

2 A Force to be reckoned with Jane Robinson. Virago 2011
A modern history of the WI – excellent.

3 Rooms off the Corridor Anne Stamper NFWI. 1998
A superb detailed history of education in the WI including Denman College – a classic text.

4 Extraordinary Women: A history of the Women's Institutes Gwen Garner. NFWI 1995

5 Jam and Jerusalem: A pictorial history of the WI Simon Goodenough. Collins 1977

6 Adelaide Hoodless: Woman with a Vision Ruth Howes. Self-published 1965

7 Lady Denman 1884 – 1954 Gervas Huxley. Chatto and Windus 1961

8 Grace Hadow Helena Deneke. Oxford University Press 1946

9 Child of the Theatre Elizabeth Brunner. Perpetua 2010

10 Looking back from the Nineties Cicely McCall. Gliddon Books, Norwich 1994
A magnificent autobiography.

11 The First Women's Institute School 1918 Mrs Alfred Watt and Miss Nest Lloyd.
Sussex Federation of WIs 1918
Unique publication

Published and printed by Ernest Richards, Springwood, Church Lane, Sparham, Norwich, NR9 5PP
Tel: 01362 688075

Printed in Great Britain
by Amazon